Fun with Opposites
Light and Dark

by Amy McDonald

BELLWETHER MEDIA • MINNEAPOLIS, MN

Blastoff! Beginners are developed by literacy experts and educators to meet the needs of early readers. These engaging informational texts support young children as they begin reading about their world. Through simple language and high frequency words paired with crisp, colorful photos, Blastoff! Beginners launch young readers into the universe of independent reading.

Sight Words in This Book 🔍

a	each	make	this
be	has	may	to
can	in	our	we
day	is	see	you
do	it	the	your

This edition first published in 2026 by Bellwether Media, Inc.

No part of this publication may be reproduced in whole or in part without written permission of the publisher. For information regarding permission, write to Bellwether Media, Inc., Attention: Permissions Department, 3500 American Blvd W, Suite 150, Bloomington, MN 55431.

Library of Congress Cataloging-in-Publication Data

LC record for Light and Dark available at: https://lccn.loc.gov/2025003231

Text copyright © 2026 by Bellwether Media, Inc. BLASTOFF! BEGINNERS and associated logos are trademarks and/or registered trademarks of Bellwether Media, Inc. Bellwether Media is a division of FlutterBee Education Group.

Editor: Rebecca Sabelko   Designer: Laura Sowers

Printed in the United States of America, North Mankato, MN.

Table of Contents

Camping	4
Two Opposites	6
Light and Dark Things	12
Light and Dark Facts	22
Glossary	23
To Learn More	24
Index	24

Camping

Our **campsite** is dark. This fire gives us light!

campsite

Two Opposites

Light is **energy** you can see. Dark has less energy.

light

Light makes it easier to see.
It may be bright!

Dark means less light.
It is harder to see.

Light and Dark Things

The sun brings light each day. Night is darker.

night

Light shines in this dark cave.

The flashlight is bright. We make **shadows**.

flashlight

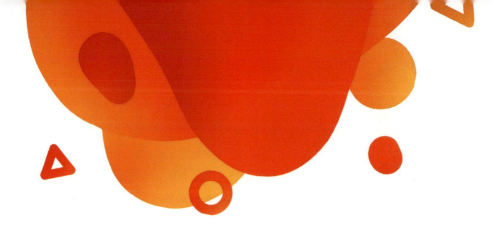

Lightning **flashes** through dark clouds.

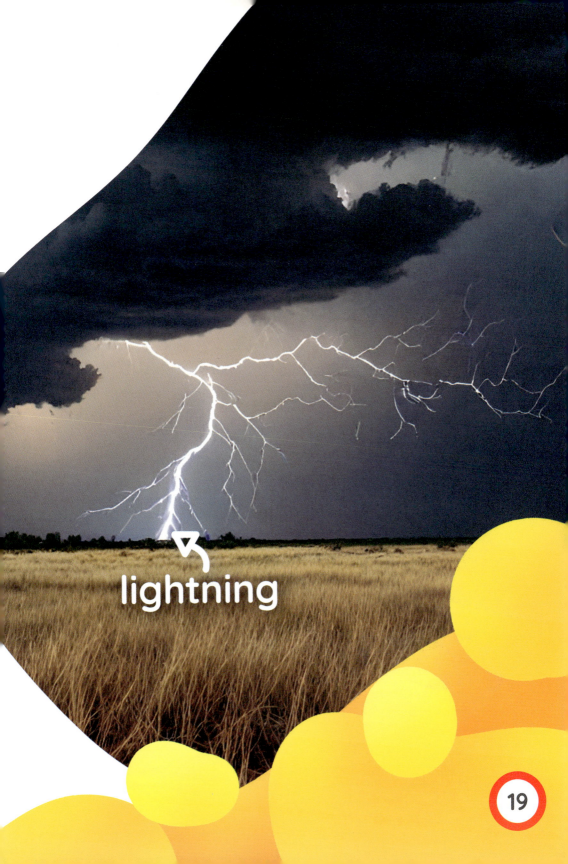

Your room is dark. Do you need a night-light?

Light and Dark Facts

Light and Dark Around Us

dark sky

light from fire

light from lantern

Something Light and Dark

day

night

Glossary

campsite

a place for camping

energy

the power to be able to do things

flashes

lights up suddenly

shadows

shapes made by blocking light

To Learn More

ON THE WEB

FACTSURFER

Factsurfer.com gives you a safe, fun way to find more information.

1. Go to www.factsurfer.com.

2. Enter "light and dark" into the search box and click 🔍.

3. Select your book cover to see a list of related content.

Index

campsite, 4, 5
cave, 14
clouds, 18
day, 12
energy, 6
fire, 4
flashes, 18
flashlight, 16
lightning, 18, 19
night, 12
night-light, 20
room, 20
see, 6, 8, 10
shadows, 16, 17
sun, 12

The images in this book are reproduced through the courtesy of: fotostoker, front cover; tr3gin, front cover; nokkaew, p. 3; Serhii Bobyk, pp. 4-5; Virrage Images, pp. 6-7; ArtEvent ET, pp. 8-9; LIGHTFIELD STUDIOS, pp. 10-11; Daniele COSSU, p. 12; Creative Travel Projects, pp. 12-13; skynesher, pp. 14-15; Bored Photography, p. 16; SanyaSM, pp. 16-17; Hasantha Lakmal, pp. 18-19; famveldman, pp. 20-21; Dpongvit, p. 22 (top); ABCDstock, p. 22 (day); Ricardo Reitmeyer, p. 22 (night); FXQuadro, p. 23 (campsite); sirirak kaewgorn, p. 23 (energy); Edgar Martirosyan, p. 23 (flashes); Pixel-Shot, p. 23 (shadows).